# BOOK ANALYSIS

By Steve MacGregor

# I, Robot
## by Isaac Asimov

Bright Summaries.com

# Shed new light on your favorite books with

Bright
≡Summaries.com

www.brightsummaries.com

# ISAAC ASIMOV 9

# *I, ROBOT* 13

# SUMMARY 17

Introduction
Robbie
Runaround
Reason
Catch That Rabbit
Liar!
Little Lost Robot
Escape!
Evidence
The Evitable Conflict

# CHARACTER STUDY 29

Dr. Susan Calvin
Mike Donovan and Gregory Powell
Stephen Byerly
The robots

# ANALYSIS 35

A positive future
Future history
Impact

# FURTHER REFLECTION 43

# FURTHER READING 47

# ISAAC ASIMOV

## AMERICAN WRITER AND PROFESSOR OF BIOCHEMISTRY

- **Born in Smolensk Oblast, Russia in 1919 or 1920 (Asimov was uncertain of the actual date and year of his birth).**
- **Died in New York City in 1992.**
- **Notable works:**
  - *Foundation* (1951), science-fiction novel
  - *The Bicentennial Man and Other Stories* (1976), short story collection
  - *Isaac Asimov's Guide to Earth and Space* (1991), non-fiction work covering astronomy and space science

Isaac Asimov was born in Russia shortly after the Russian Revolution. His Jewish family emigrated to the United States when he was three years old. Asimov gained a Master's degree in chemistry in 1941 and became a full professor of biochemistry at Boston University School of Medicine in 1978. However, he is best remembered as one of the most prolific writers of what has become known as the Golden Age of Science Fiction. Asimov wrote or edited more than five hundred books and a vast number of short stories. Many were science fiction tales, though he also wrote science textbooks and fiction in other genres.

Some of Asimov's science fiction works have come to be regarded as classics of the genre and a number have influenced subsequent writers. Asimov combined his own knowledge of emerging sciences with a fascination for the interaction between humans and machines to produce works that were both prophetic and thoughtful. Asimov is regarded as one of the most important science fiction writers and won every major science fiction literary award during his lifetime.

# *I, ROBOT*

## A HISTORY OF THE NEAR FUTURE

- **Genre:** thematically linked short story collection
- **Reference edition:** Asimov, I. (2018) *I, Robot*. London: Harper Collins.
- **1st edition:** 1950
- **Themes:** human/machine interaction, morality, free will, emotion, self-awareness, ethics, creation, control

By the early 1940s, Isaac Asimov was a regular contributor to popular science fiction magazines including *Astounding Science Fiction* and *Super Science Stories*. These 'pulp' magazines (so-called because they were generally printed on inexpensive paper made from wood-pulp) were extremely popular in America in the 1930s and 1940s and often included short stories by writers who would go on to become some of the most significant names in science fiction. Asimov had written a series of stories which dealt with the relationship between humans and humanoid machines – robots. Asimov wrote these stories as history, as if they were written in the future and looking back at the development of robots. In 1949, Asimov was persuaded to release nine of these short stories as an anthology.

To tie the stories together, Asimov added an introduction and elements of a framing narrative so that each story became part of an interview being conducted by a reporter for the Interplanetary Press in the year 2058. The subject is the chief robopsychologist at U.S. Robots and Mechanical Men, Inc., Dr. Susan Calvin, on the occasion of her retirement. Each of the stories is presented as an anecdote told by Dr. Calvin, with additional narrative by the reporter to provide context. The book begins with a preface, a quotation from the fictional 56$^{th}$ (2058) edition of the *Handbook of Robotics,* which states the *Three Laws of Robotics.* These are:

- **First Law**: A robot may not injure a human being, or, through inaction, allow a human being to come to harm.
- **Second Law**: A robot must obey the orders given it by human beings except where such orders would conflict with the First Law.

- **Third Law**: A robot must protect its own existence as long as such protection does not conflict with the First or Second Laws.

# SUMMARY

## INTRODUCTION

The short introduction to this work is provided by an unnamed reporter for the Interplanetary Press who has been given the assignment of interviewing Dr. Susan Calvin, one of the foremost scientists involved in the design and production of robots. The interview takes place on the occasion of Dr. Calvin's retirement in 2058, by which time robots have become completely integrated into everyday life on Earth and on the other planets colonised by humans. The reporter wants her to look back over her long career and to provide readers with some insight into her life and work. However, Dr. Calvin is reluctant to talk about herself and instead chooses to give an account of her career and the increasing importance of robots by telling nine stories, each of which illustrates an aspect of the history of the development of robots and their relationships with humans.

# ROBBIE

On Earth in 1998, a nine-year-old girl, Gloria Weston, is playing hide-and-seek with her favorite household robot, Robbie. This robot is a relatively primitive model in some ways – it cannot speak, for example, and it is able to communicate only by gesture, but it is sufficiently aware that it understands both the rules of this game and that Gloria badly wants to win, though the robot's sensors mean that it is always aware of Gloria's location. The robot allows Gloria to win and it become clear that this is the little girl's favourite playmate.

However, Gloria's mother, Grace, does not entirely trust the machine and is nervous about the amount of time her daughter is spending in the robot's company, so she persuades her husband George to have Robbie returned to the factory in which he was manufactured. Gloria is very upset, and in order to distract her, the family buy her a puppy which she compares unfavourably to Robbie: "I don't want the nasty dog – I want Robbie." (Chapter 2 – *Robbie*). The family then take a trip to New York City, where they visit the factory of U.S. Robots and Mechanical Men, Inc., the only manufacturer of robots. Gloria's father believes that if she sees robots being created, she will understand that they are only machines and will stop pining for Robbie. While touring the factory, Gloria sees Robbie, who is now working on a production line, and rushes to greet him. She runs into the path of a moving vehicle and is only saved when Robbie sees what is happening and snatches her from under the wheels of the approaching tractor. The family are so grateful that they agree to take Robbie back into their home.

## RUNAROUND

This story is set on the planet Mercury in the year 2015 and is the first to deal with the laws of robotics. Two mining engineers, Mike Donovan and Gregory Powell, are stranded on Mercury and in order to keep their life-support equipment running, they need additional supplies of selenium. However, collecting this material is very dangerous and they send out their only functioning robot, SPD 13, to collect a small quantity of selenium. The robot fails to return and the two men are forced out onto the planet's surface to find it. They discover that the robot's positronic brain has become confused by the need to follow the conflicting demands of the three laws of robotics.

SPD 13 has been given orders to retrieve the selenium (in accordance with the Second Law), but this will place it in danger (thus breaking the Third Law). The robot's simplistic reasoning is unable to cope with this confusion and it moves back and forth beside the pool of selenium, not close enough to harm itself but not close enough to retrieve a sample either. Gregory Powell resolves the problem by deliberately placing himself in danger, thus causing the robot to break the loop and save him, obeying the First Law. The two engineers are then able to tell SPD 13 that gathering the selenium will save their lives, and because this invokes the First Law the robot returns and retrieves the vital sample without problems.

## REASON

This story is also set in 2015 and once again features Donovan and Powell, now based on a space station. A new, more advanced robot, QT-1 (Cutie), arrives and immediately causes problems.

Cutie has improved reasoning ability and comes to believe that it is innately superior to humans. For this reason, it refuses to accept that it could have been created by humans and becomes unwilling to take orders from Donovan and Powell. A dangerous electron storm is approaching which will cause devastation on Earth unless the engineers are able to adjust the energy beam which is focussed from the space station.

Cutie at first refuses to allow them to adjust the beam, but is finally persuaded when it becomes apparent that all robots, no matter how advanced or how superior they believe themselves to be, must obey the Second Law – to follow direct orders given by humans.

## CATCH THAT RABBIT

Set the following year, this story sees Donovan and Powell on a small asteroid overseeing the activities of yet another new robot, DV-5 (Dave), a mining robot which in turn controls six less sophisticated sub-robots. Dave becomes increasingly erratic and it takes a near disaster before Gregory Powell realises that having six subordinates to control is placing too much stress on the robot's relatively simple positronic brain, causing it to act in bizarre ways. Powell reduces the stress by destroying one of the sub-robots and Dave is restored to normal operation.

## LIAR!

Back on Earth, in 2021, US Robotics accidentally creates a robot, RB-34 (Herbie), which can read human minds. Herbie becomes aware that Susan Calvin is in love with another scientist at the factory, Milton Ashe. When Ashe brings another woman to the plant for a visit, Calvin is devastated, but Herbie assures her that the woman is only Ashe's cousin. Later, Calvin discovers that this is not true – the woman is Ashe's fiancée and Herbie has lied to protect her feelings.

Later, Dr. Calvin asks the robot what it was that made it able to read minds. The robot is unable to answer, because it believes that doing so will harm a human by making them feel bad because a robot understands something that they do not, but this breaks the Second Law because it is failing to respond to a direct order from a human. Unable to resolve this conflict, Herbie shuts down and is irrevocably damaged.

# LITTLE LOST ROBOT

In 2029, Dr. Calvin is summoned to Hyper Base, a centre of transport and mining, to investigate a missing robot. The robot is a new NS-2 (Nestor) model which has been modified to make it more suitable for mining operations – within its positronic brain the First Law had been changed to remove the clause preventing a human being harmed by the robot's inaction because mining operations require humans to occasionally place themselves in hazardous situations. This makes it potentially dangerous, but there are 63 identical Nestors at the base and Dr. Calvin's assignment is to identify the one which has been modified.

She tries several tests, all of which fail to identify the modified robot. Finally, she discovers that the modified robot has been provided with a superior knowledge of etheric physics and she uses this to expose the modified robot, who attempts to attack her. As the robot advances towards her, the room is bathed in gamma rays, which are harmless to humans but fatal to positronic brains, and the robot is destroyed. It is agreed that there will be no further attempts to modify the First Law.

# ESCAPE!

In 2030, scientists are attempting to build a space craft with a hyperspace drive. Robots are required to design the ship and its drive system, but this causes problems because the drive is potentially harmful to humans, generating a conflict between the First and Second Laws of robotics. Dr. Calvin instructs a highly advanced robot, *The Brain,* to design the ship and Mike Donovan and Gregory Powell are sent out on the first hyperspace trip.

Both suffer near-death experiences during the trip - both are technically dead for a short time, though both recover. Dr. Calvin explains how she was able to modify *The Brain*'s understanding of the First Law to ignore temporary death and thus complete the design of the ship.

# EVIDENCE

In 2032, a man named Stephen Byerly runs for political office on Earth. However, there are persistent rumours that Byerly is actually a robot – by this time, the construction of robots is so sophisticated that it is impossible to tell them apart from humans. Dr. Calvin is called in to make a judgement.

She asks Byerly to hit another man, which he does, thus demonstrating that he cannot be a robot because this would have contravened the First Law. However, Calvin is later forced to admit that it is possible that the person he struck may also have been a robot, so that the test could have been worthless. Calvin confesses that even she cannot be absolutely certain whether or not Byerly is a robot, but adds that she does not feel that this is important.

## THE EVITABLE CONFLICT

By 2052, Stephen Byerly has become *World Co-ordinator*, effectively the ruler of Earth and the colonised worlds. Robots now control most aspects of planning and production, and these generally proceed without any problems. However, a small, secret cabal of powerful men, the Society for Humanity, has started to interfere with this planning, causing occasional problems. Dr. Calvin is called in to investigate.

However, she is able to assure Byerly that the robots which now control the world are not only aware of this secret society, but they use the data they derive from its actions to ensure that their control is total and that things such as wars, famine and economic disruption are now avoidable, or "evitable". Dr. Calvin concludes, "Only the Machines, from now on, are inevitable!" (Chapter 9 – *The Evitable Conflict*).

# CHARACTER STUDY

## DR. SUSAN CALVIN

Each chapter is presented as a story told by Dr. Susan Calvin, and she appears as a character in six of them. She is portrayed as completely involved in her work as a robopsychologist for U.S. Robots and Mechanical Men, Inc. She is logical and shows almost no emotion in any of these stories – in an early exchange with the reporter who is interviewing her, she tells him: "Well, I've been called a robot myself. Surely, they've told you I'm not human" (*Introduction*). The only exception is the story *Liar!*, in which she admits to having feelings for a younger colleague, though these are not reciprocated.

In several of these stories, Dr. Calvin uses deduction and the application of logic to solve the problems she is presented with. However, even her title is a contradiction – robots do not have psychology in the human sense; their positronic brains are programmed and her role is simply to understand and interpret that programming.

There is an implication that Dr. Calvin herself has come to think like one of her robots.

The character of Dr. Calvin subverted many of the conventions of science fiction in the 1940s. First and most notably, she is a woman, and female protagonists were virtually unknown in this period. Second, she uses reason rather than force to achieve her goals, and this was very unusual in a time when most science fiction involved tough male characters who used weapons and brute strength to overcome difficulties.

## MIKE DONOVAN AND GREGORY POWELL

These two engineers appear in four of these stories and are much closer to the science fiction archetypes of the 1940s. They are wise-cracking, brave men of action who tend to tackle problems head-on, though it is clear that both are also intelligent and well trained. The red-haired Donovan tends to lose his temper and is occasionally intemperate – for example, he threatens to hit Cutie if he does not do as he is instructed in *Reason*. In the same story, Powell attempts to reason with the robot.

This double-act of the calm and reasonable Powell and the hot-tempered Donovan is used to provide comic relief in several stories. Both characters also work for U.S. Robots and Mechanical Men, Inc. and are colleagues of Dr. Calvin, who they appear to respect.

## STEPHEN BYERLY

Bylerly appears in only the last two stories. In the first, *Evidence*, he is a rising politician; in the second, *The Evitable Conflict*, he has become the World Co-ordinator. In the first story, the plot hinges on the question of whether or not Byerly is a robot, but this question is never completely answered. When the reporter asks Dr. Calvin to clarify this point, she answers: "Oh, there's no way of ever finding out. I think he was" (Chapter 8 – *Evidence*). It is clear that Dr. Calvin is comfortable with the notion of a robot assuming a position of power because robots are controlled by the Three Laws, whereas humans are unpredictable.

In the final story, *The Evitable Conflict*, the question of whether Byerly is or is not a robot is ignored, though his calm understanding and acceptance of the fact that robots now control every aspect of human existence suggests that he may be.

## THE ROBOTS

The stories which form this book are placed in chronological order in terms of the dates in which they are set. Throughout the stories we see the robots progressing from the relatively unsophisticated Robbie in the first story, who lacks even the ability for speech, to the robots of the final stories, who are indistinguishable from human beings and have been given control over virtually every aspect of human life.

In general, the robots in these stories are portrayed in a very positive way and any issues they may have are attributable to human intervention and frailty. Robots are dedicated to making the lives of their human masters better and safer, and they are unencumbered by egos, desires or ambition. They are, as Dr. Calvin tells the reporter, "a cleaner, better breed than we are" (*Introduction*).

# ANALYSIS

These are science fiction stories, a genre characterised by:

- a futuristic, often dystopian setting;
- advanced technology;
- locations other than Earth;
- alien species.

In terms of the first three of these points, these stories generally fit well, though there is nothing dystopian about the future envisaged by Asimov. In terms of the last point, they do not fit at all, and that was one of the things that made Isaac Asimov's writing unusual in the 1940s. While most contemporary science fiction writers introduced alien creatures and worlds, which were often hostile, there are no aliens in these stories and very few in any of Asimov's other stories or novels. Asimov used his science fiction to focus on the human condition rather than esoteric new worlds or impressive gadgets. In 1953, he published an essay in which he noted that science fiction writing generally fitted into one of three categories, *Gadget, Adventure* or *Social*. *Gadget* stories focussed on technology, *Adventure* was action-based, while *Social* stories looked at how changes in the future might affect humans. While most science fiction at that time fell into one of the first two categories, Asimov focussed almost exclusively on social science fiction.

At the time *I, Robot* was published, it stood out because of the philosophical approach of most of its stories and because the protagonists mainly used intelligence and logic to resolve their problems. *I, Robot* is not just a collection of stories about an imagined future – it is a wider rumination on the relationship between humans and the machines they create, and this may help to explain why it has remained so popular.

Asimov took the opportunity to edit the text of the original stories to make them fit together better before they were published as *I, Robot*. He had also continually refined and changed the Three Laws of Robotics as these stories were originally published, but in this anthology he took the opportunity to present the definitive version of these laws and provided these as a preface. The Laws are important here because they form a significant element of the plot of several of the stories.

# A POSITIVE FUTURE

Asimov was himself a scientist and he was able to see how advances in science might affect humanity. In the decade before the publication of this work, the world had been introduced to frightening new technology including nuclear weapons, guided missiles and computers. It was clear that a future that featured these new technologies would be very different, and Asimov was one of the few writers to use science fiction to examine what this future might look like and how people might respond to it. A recurring theme in these stories is that robots are more reliable and more consistent than humans. In each case, a problem with a robot can be traced to a human failure. However, in almost every story, humans prove to be more intelligent than their robot creations, outwitting malfunctioning robots by using superior intelligence. However, it is notable that in many stories, the intelligence that solves the problem comes from Dr. Calvin, who is herself described as being cold and emotionless, like a robot.

Overall, the tone of these stories is positive. Robots are seen as providing real benefits to humanity and are dedicated to protecting it, unlike many contemporary works where technology is seen as a threat. Asimov believed that improving technology was inevitable and he understood that many people felt threatened by this. One of the purposes of his work was to provide reassurance that a technological future could be a better place with new inventions improving the lives of humans.

## FUTURE HISTORY

Asimov read *The History of the Decline and Fall of the Roman Empire* by Edward Gibbon (English writer and historian, 1737 – 1794) a short time before writing the first story in this collection. He was hugely impressed by this work and decided that he wanted to produce a series of stories about the near future, written as though by a historian looking back at them. The result was the chronological series of stories which became *I, Robot*, in each of which Dr. Calvin is allowed the benefit of hindsight to place the events of each tale in its proper historical context. This framing narrative was not included when the stories were originally and individually published in science fiction magazines but was added when Asimov was later persuaded to bring them together as a linked series.

Asimov originally wanted to call this collection *Mind and Iron*, but his publisher persuaded him to accept *I, Robot* instead. This was also the title of a 1939 short story by Eando Binder published in *Amazing Stories* magazine. Asimov read that story and later said that it inspired him to begin writing *Robbie*, which became the first of the *I, Robot* chapters, in 1940.

## IMPACT

*I, Robot* exemplifies many themes of the so-called Golden Age of Science Fiction, which is generally accepted to have been from 1938 to the late 1950s. This writing extolled technology as a cure for many of the ills which afflicted mankind and after 1945, and science fiction was increasingly adopted by mainstream publishers who had previously avoided the genre. The first edition of *I, Robot* was published in 1950 by Gnome Press, a small New York publisher, in an edition of only 5000 copies. In 1956 it was republished by Signet Press, another New York publisher, as a mass-market paperback. By 1963, science fiction had become sufficiently respectable that *I, Robot* was published by Doubleday, a mainstream New York publishing house. Until books like *I, Robot*, science fiction was so little regarded that it was very difficult for writers in this genre to make a living – prolific as he was, even Asimov treated his writing as a hobby until 1958, when he was finally able to earn enough to become a professional writer.

Asimov's scholarly approach to writing helped to make science fiction acceptable to a mass market and to be viewed as legitimate literature for the first time. During the 1960s this new-found acceptance led directly to the emergence of the New Wave movement in science fiction writing, where there was increased experimentation in both literary form and content. Isaac Asimov was instrumental in changing the way in which science fiction was regarded, and *I, Robot* was one of the books that led to this change.

Asimov returned to the robots envisaged in this collection in many other works. In all, Asimov wrote 29 other short stories which featured robots and the Three Laws of Robotics, though none included Dr. Susan Calvin or other characters from these stories. He also wrote a series of four linked novels which further explored the relationship between humans and humanoid robots in the distant future. Asimov was a keen reader (and later, writer) of mystery stories, and these four novels, *The Caves of Steel* (1953), *The Naked Sun* (1955), *The Robots of Dawn* (1983) and *Robots and Empire* (1985), are all stories of investigations carried out by detective Elijah Baley and his humanoid robot partner R. Daneel Olivaw. These novels are set thousands of years after the stories of *I, Robot*, but they share many of the same themes, namely the Three Laws of Robotics, the interaction between machines and humans and the extent to which robots are more effective at controlling human destiny than humans themselves. These four novels, *I, Robot* and the other 29 short stories are generally referred to as the *'Robot Series'* and the final novel, *Robots and Empire*, links this series with Asimov's other great science fiction saga, the *Foundation* series.

# **FURTHER REFLECTION**

## SOME QUESTIONS TO THINK ABOUT...

- Dr. Calvin claims that robots are "a cleaner, better breed than we are" (*Introduction*). Do you agree?
- "Think, that for all time, all conflicts are finally evitable. Only the Machines, from now on, are inevitable!" (Chapter 9 – *The Evitable Conflict*). Do you think that giving total control of human affairs to robots would be a good idea? Why/why not?
- Asimov rarely described technology in detail in his writing – for example, the "positronic brain" is mentioned several times in these stories, but there is no attempt to describe it or explain how it works. Why do you think he did this?
- Though several of these stories take place on other planets or space stations, there is no mention of alien life-forms. Why do you think Asimov chose not to have aliens in these stories?

- The stories in this collection were originally written as separate tales and only later re-worked and provided with additional framing narrative to link them together. Does this work? Are there any stories that do not seem to belong here?
- In these stories, the robots generally refer to humans as "master" and humans often call robots "boy." What do you think about this?
- "The Machine cannot, must not, make us unhappy" (Chapter 9 – *The Evitable Conflict*). These stories generally take an optimistic view of the impact of technology on human affairs. Do you think that these stories would use the same tone if they were written today? Why/why not?
- Do you think that Dr. Susan Calvin may actually be a robot? Why/why not?

*We want to hear from you!*
*Leave a comment on your online library*
*and share your favourite books on social media!*

# FURTHER READING

## REFERENCE EDITION

- Asimov, I. (2018) *I, Robot*. London: Harper Collins.

## ADDITIONAL SOURCES

- Asimov, I. (1979) *In Memory Yet Green: The Autobiography of Isaac Asimov, 1920-1954*. New York: Doubleday.
- White, M. (2005) *Isaac Asimov: A Life of the Grand Master of Science Fiction*. Boston: De Capo Press.

## ADAPTATIONS

- There have been several television adaptations of stories from this collection. The first was an episode based on *Little Lost Robot* included in the British science fiction anthology series *Out of This World*, hosted by actor Boris Karloff and first broadcast in 1962. Another British science fiction anthology series, *Out of the Unknown*, included two episodes based on *Reason* and *Liar!* from this collection. An episode of the Russian science fiction series *This Fantastic World* titled *Don't Joke with Robots* and broadcast in 1987 was also partly based on *Liar!*

- Science fiction writer Harlan Ellison was commissioned in 1977 by Warner Brothers to write a screenplay based on *I, Robot*. Asimov was reported as being very happy with this adaptation, but the film was never made. Ellison's screenplay was released in 1994 as *I, Robot, The Illustrated Screenplay* (Norwalk: Easton Press).

- In 2004 a film starring Will Smith was released but, though it used the title *I, Robot*, it had very little to do with this collection. The film did use some plot elements from *Little Lost Robot* (as well as the later Asimov robot novel *The Caves of Steel*) and mentions the Three Laws of Robotics, but it is otherwise completely different in tone and content to Asimov's writing – the film, for example, features killer robots who plan to overthrow their human masters.

- In 2010 Mickey Zucker Reichert (American science fiction and fantasy writer, 1962-) was commissioned by the estate of Isaac Asimov to write three prequel novels to *I, Robot*. *I Robot: To Protect* was published in 2011 and was followed by *I Robot: To Obey* in 2013 and *I Robot: To Preserve* in 2016 (New York: Berkley Books).

- The British Broadcasting Corporation (BBC) aired five 15-minute radio dramas on Radio 4 based on stories from this collection (*Robbie, Reason, Little Lost Robot, Liar!* and *The Evitable Conflict*) in 2017.

# Bright ≡Summaries.com

## More guides to rediscover your love of literature

**Animal Farm**
BY GEORGE ORWELL

**The Stranger**
BY ALBERT CAMUS

**Harry Potter and the Sorcerer's Stone**
BY J.K. ROWLING

**The Silence of the Sea**
BY VERCORS

**Antigone**
BY JEAN ANOUILH

**The Flowers of Evil**
BY BAUDELAIRE

www.brightsummaries.com

Although the editor makes every effort to verify the accuracy of the information published, BrightSummaries.com accepts no responsibility for the content of this book.

**© BrightSummaries.com, 2019. All rights reserved.**

www.brightsummaries.com

Ebook EAN: 9782808017145

Paperback EAN: 9782808017152

Legal Deposit: D/2019/12603/24

Cover: © Primento

Digital conception by Primento, the digital partner of publishers.

Made in the
USA
Monee, IL